On The Beach

by Meish Goldish

illustrated by Bob Berry

Harcourt
SCHOOL PUBLISHERS

Printed in the United States of America

ISBN 10: 0-15-351694-1
ISBN 13: 978-0-15-351694-8

Ordering Options
ISBN 10: 0-15-351216-4 (Grade 6 Advanced Collection)
ISBN 13: 978-0-15-351216-2 (Grade 6 Advanced Collection)
ISBN 10: 0-15-358177-8 (package of 5)
ISBN 13: 978-0-15-358177-9 (package of 5)

2 3 4 5 6 7 8 9 10   179   12 11 10 09 08 07

Malcolm walked with an extra bounce in his step. He looked forward to an exciting morning at the beach. The California sun was shining brightly. A pleasant breeze blew across the sandy shore. Inland, tall blades of grass danced in the wind. Malcolm sensed it was an ideal day to collect seashells.

"You look as happy as a clam," Lewis huffed, trying to keep up with Malcolm.

"Which kind of clam do you mean?" Malcolm joked. "A hard-shell clam or a soft-shell clam? A giant clam or a razor clam?"

Lewis laughed. "Whichever kind of clam is happiest," he said, to which he added, "Mister Show-off!"

Lewis was Malcolm's best friend. He knew he could tease Malcolm, especially about clams. After all, clams had shells, and shells were something Malcolm knew all about. He'd been collecting them since he was six years old. Now, five years later, he had hundreds of shells in his collection.

Malcolm didn't just collect shells, however. He would make special labels for each one. He wrote down the name of the shell. He wrote down when and where he found it. At home, he washed and polished each shell. Finally, he chose a special place for it on one of the shelves in his home. Malcolm jokingly called them his "shells shelves."

Lewis looked at the canvas bag that Malcolm carried over his shoulder. "How many shells did you bring today?" he asked.

"Twenty-five," Malcolm replied. Whenever Malcolm visited the beach, he brought sample shells from his collection. He didn't like to collect new shells that were too similar to ones he already had. After finding a new shell, he'd check it against the ones in his bag. If they looked too much alike, he'd toss the new shell.

"I'll bet you have the best seashell collection in Sanibel Island," Lewis said as they approached the beach. "Hundreds of shells, and no two are exactly alike. That's amazing."

"It's a good collection," Malcolm agreed, "but it's not perfect."

"What would make it perfect?" Lewis asked.

Malcolm said, "I'd love to have a giant clam shell from the South Pacific Ocean. Do you know how big they can be? Four feet (1.2 m) long! That's as big as we are. Also, they can weigh 500 pounds (227 kg)."

"That's bigger than both of us!" Lewis laughed. At last, the boys reached the beach. Immediately, they began to search near the water for shells. The two worked quietly for many minutes. Malcolm had taught Lewis that finding good shells took concentration.

Malcolm didn't just seek out large shells. He hunted for smaller ones as well. Some shells in his collection came from sea snails. Many were the size of a fingernail. Malcolm knew that sea snail shells could be even smaller than that. Some were as tiny as a grain of sand!

The two boys searched in the wet sand. At first, they found mostly sticks and pebbles. Then Malcolm came across an empty juice can that someone had left on the ground.

"This really annoys me," Malcolm blurted out, breaking the silence. He picked up the can and tossed it into a nearby trash bin. "I wish people would treat the beach with more respect," he sighed sadly.

"Maybe you should collect cans, too," Lewis joked.

Suddenly, Malcolm saw something move in the sand in front of him. At first, he couldn't tell what it was. Then the movement stopped, and Malcolm bent down to examine further.

"Lewis, come here!" he called out. "I found a crab!"

Lewis hurried over. Together, the boys looked closely at the ground. There was the crab, wedged between two large, flat rocks. Malcolm feared the crab might be trapped. Maybe it was injured, he thought. However, the crab crawled out suddenly and scrambled atop one of the rocks.

"Cool!" Lewis cried with joy. "I've never seen a live crab before. Are they dangerous?"

"No," Malcolm laughed, "although I wouldn't want to shake hands with one. Their claws are pretty sharp, and they cling tightly. Watch this."

Malcolm found a long, thin stick nearby. He pushed the far end gently between the crab's claws. The crab gripped the stick. Malcolm lifted it about a foot off the ground. The crab remained attached to the stick.

"See?" Malcolm said. "A free elevator ride."

Malcolm lowered the stick to the ground. The crab let go and slunk around the two rocks. The two boys watched the little creature with great interest.

"What kind of crab is it?" Lewis asked. "Are all crabs pretty much the same?"

"Hardly!" Malcolm replied. "This one is too big to be a pea crab, yet it's much too small to be an Alaska king crab." Malcolm paused to study the creature. Then he added, "I believe this is a hermit crab."

Lewis smiled. "A hermit crab?" he said. "Sounds like a lonely character to me!"

Malcolm nodded his head. "You're right," he agreed. "A hermit crab lives all alone."

"Where does it live?" Lewis joked. "In a tiny log cabin deep in the woods?"

Malcolm shook his head. "Very funny," he replied, smiling. "Actually, it lives inside the shell of a sea snail."

Lewis looked confused. "Inside a snail's shell?" Lewis asked. "How can it live with a snail? I thought you said a hermit crab lives alone."

"It does live alone," Malcolm explained. "It only moves into the shell after the snail has died, unless it's a fighter, of course. Then the hermit crab will actually pull a live snail out of its shell, just so the crab can move in."

"That doesn't sound fair," Lewis said. "The crab should pick on someone its own size."

"Sometimes it does," Malcolm said, laughing. "Sometimes a hermit crab will pull another crab out of a shell that it wants."

Lewis shook his head. "No wonder crabs are so crabby," he joked. "They never know when they're going to lose their home!"

"Yes," Malcolm agreed. "However, this crab is searching for a home, not losing one."

Lewis snapped his fingers. "I've got an idea!" he cried. "Let's find this hermit crab a new home."

Lewis looked around on the sand. Soon he saw a seashell near the ocean waters. He brought it to Malcolm, who examined the shell and handed it back to Lewis.

"A hermit crab won't want this," Malcolm said. "It's an oyster shell. We need to find a sea snail shell."

"I don't think a crab really knows the difference," Lewis said. "Here, I'll show you." He placed the oyster shell on the sand, about a foot from the hermit crab.

"Come on, Hermit," Lewis said to the crab. "Here's a new home for you. Go on inside."

The hermit crab crawled away from the shell. It perched itself on top of one of the rocks.

"I told you it wouldn't want it as a home," Malcolm said.

"It's a perfectly nice shell," Lewis exclaimed. He picked it up and handed it to Malcolm. "Well," he sighed, "since Hermit doesn't want it, you may as well add it to your collection."

Malcolm returned the shell to Lewis. "Thanks, but I can't use it," Malcolm explained. "I've already got an oyster shell that looks just like it. In fact, I think I brought it here today." He opened his shell bag and pulled out an oyster shell. Sure enough, the two shells looked liked twins.

Suddenly, Lewis had an idea. "Malcolm," he asked, "is there a sea snail shell in your bag?"

Malcolm gave Lewis a serious look. "Yes, there is, but I want to keep it for my collection," he replied. "I'm not giving it to the hermit crab."

Lewis said, "Fine. I'll look for another sea snail shell on the beach. I want poor Hermit to have a home."

Malcolm and Lewis continued their search. Only now, they had two different goals. Malcolm was searching for shells for his collection. Lewis was looking for a shell for the hermit crab.

The boys combed the beach for several more minutes. Suddenly, Lewis called, "Malcolm, look what I found!"

Malcolm ran over, hoping to see a new shell. Instead, Lewis was holding a large glass jar.

"More trash!" Malcolm grunted. "I can't believe what people leave around here."

"It's not trash," Lewis replied. "This jar would make a great home for Hermit." He took the jar and carried it back to the two flat rocks. Malcolm followed. To Malcolm's surprise, the hermit crab was still perched on one of the rocks.

Malcolm shook his head slowly. "This is not going to work, Lewis," he said. "I told you, a hermit crab lives only in the shell of a sea snail. It's not going to move into a glass jar."

"Why not?" Lewis asked. "The jar will protect Hermit. He'll never have to worry about being pelted by rain. We could decorate it with sand and pebbles. Hermit will love his new home. It'll be like having a house on the beach!"

Malcolm shook his head again. "I know you don't want to leave the crab stranded on the beach, but it'll find its own home. It's not going to settle for your jar. It won't even crawl inside."

"We'll see about that," Lewis said. He took the stick that Malcolm had used earlier. He got the crab to grasp hold of it, and then he lowered the crab into the mouth of the jar.

"Now let go of the stick, Hermit," Lewis said. "Welcome to your new home."

The boys watched closely. The crab continued to cling to the stick. "I told you it would refuse your home," Malcolm said.

Lewis lifted the stick out of the jar. Back on the ground, the crab let go of the stick and crawled away. Lewis watched as it disappeared in the distance. "Well," he sighed, "it seemed like a good idea at the time."

Malcolm said, "I'm sorry your plan didn't work, Lewis, but have patience. Mother Nature will take her course. In time, the hermit crab will find itself a home. Meanwhile, would you like to help me search for more shells for my collection?"

Lewis shrugged his shoulders. "I guess so," he said sadly. "I may as well do something useful."

Together, the boys spent the next hour combing the sand for seashells. They found several that Malcolm liked. One was a colorful pink conch shell. Another was a white carrier shell that had smaller shells attached to it. A third was a tan-colored scallop shell. Malcolm made notes on when and where he found each shell. He planned to transfer the information to labels later.

Malcolm placed his newest shells into the canvas bag. "Okay, let's leave now," he said to Lewis. "I'm getting hungry. Want to come over to my home and have lunch with me?"

Lewis said, "Fine. At least you have a home to return to. Not like poor Hermit."

Malcolm laughed. "I told you, the crab will be just fine. It'll find its own home. Plus, it'll be a home that it really wants, too."

Malcolm took his canvas bag and slung it over his shoulder. He and Lewis didn't notice that one shell accidentally fell out of the bag and onto the ground.

At home, Malcolm and Lewis made sandwiches for lunch. After eating, Malcolm began to clean his new shells. He washed each shell with a warm, wet cloth. He got rid of all the dirt and sand that clung to each shell's surface. He even used a toothpick to pick out tiny grains of sand packed into a crevice in one of the shells. Finally, Malcolm prepared a label for each new shell.

TYPE: Conch Shell
COLOR: Pink
Date July 9, 2006
PLACE: Monterey Beach
about 2 feet (0.6 meter)
from the Ocean

TYPE: Carrier Shell
COLOR: White
DATE: July 9, 2006
PLACE: Monterey Beach
about 5 feet (1.5 meters)
from the ocean.

TYPE: Scallop Shell
COLOR: Tan
Date: July 9, 2006
Place: Monterey Beach
among the eelgrass, about
30 feet (9.1 meters) from
the Ocean

When the labels were complete, Malcolm placed them on the shelves with his new shells. He also put back the shells he had brought to the beach that morning. That's when he noticed that one shell was missing. He searched the canvas bag, but it was empty. He looked all over the floor but found nothing.

"Lewis, have you seen an extra shell lying around?" Malcolm asked. "One of mine is missing." Lewis shook his head no.

Malcolm said, "We've got to return to the beach. The shell may have fallen out of the bag. I really want to get it back."

The two boys left the house and walked quickly toward the beach. The California sun was now shining directly overhead in the sky. It smiled down on the boys as they hurried toward the shore.

Soon the boys had reached the sand. They walked to the place where Malcolm had slung the bag over his shoulder. At first, they found nothing on the ground. They walked several more feet. Suddenly, Lewis called out.

"Malcolm, look ahead!" he cried. "It's Hermit!"

Malcolm stared at the ground in front of him. There, in the sand, was the hermit crab. It was inside a sea snail shell. Malcolm could tell immediately that it was the shell he had lost earlier.

The two boys watched the crab in the shell. "I'm amazed that Hermit could squeeze in there," Lewis said.

"A hermit crab bends well," Malcolm explained. "It has a soft body that twists easily."

"His claws don't fit inside the shell," Lewis said.

"That's the way the crab likes it," Malcolm replied. "It uses its claws for a door."

"Still looks like a tight fit to me," Lewis said. "I think Hermit should have kept the glass jar for a home. It was much bigger than this snail shell."

Malcolm said, "Don't worry. When the crab grows larger, it will leave this shell and find a larger one."

Lewis asked, "You mean you're not going to take the shell away from Hermit? After all, it's from *your* shell collection."

"I know," Malcolm sighed, "but I don't have the heart to make Hermit go searching for another home. I'm happy knowing that I helped solve his problem."

"Happy?" Lewis joked. "I'll bet you're as happy as a clam!"

"Actually," Malcolm replied, "I'm as happy as a crab."

"A hermit crab!" Lewis said, laughing.

Think Critically

1. How can you tell that Malcolm values his shell collection?

2. Why does Malcolm concentrate so hard when looking for shells?

3. Why does the hermit crab reject the homes that Lewis offers it?

4. What does Malcolm mean when he tells Lewis, "Mother Nature will take her course"?

5. Do you think Malcolm should have taken back the shell that the hermit crab chose for its home? Explain.

 Science

Crabs Hermit crabs are one type of crab. Research other types of crabs on the Internet or at the library. How are the crabs different? How are they similar?

School-Home Connection Tell your family about the life of a hermit crab. Then talk about whether you would prefer to live alone or with other people. Discuss the advantages and disadvantages of each situation.

Word Count: 2,410